A Crabtree Branches Book

Today's Stars

KEVIN HART

Samantha Bell

Crabtree Publishing
crabtreebooks.com

I0800867

School-to-Home Support for Caregivers and Teachers

This high-interest book is designed to motivate striving students with engaging topics while building fluency, vocabulary, and an interest in reading. Here are a few questions and activities to help the reader build upon his or her comprehension skills.

Before Reading:

- *What do I think this book is about?*
- *What do I know about this topic?*
- *What do I want to learn about this topic?*
- *Why am I reading this book?*

During Reading:

- *I wonder why...*
- *I'm curious to know...*
- *How is this like something I already know?*
- *What have I learned so far?*

After Reading:

- *What was the author trying to teach me?*
- *What are some details?*
- *How did the photographs and captions help me understand more?*
- *Read the book again and look for the vocabulary words.*
- *What questions do I still have?*

Extension Activities:

- *What was your favorite part of the book? Write a paragraph on it.*
- *Draw a picture of your favorite thing you learned from the book.*

TABLE OF CONTENTS

FUNNY MAN

Many people recognize Kevin Hart from television or movies. He is a successful **comedian**, actor, and **producer**. They may also recognize him because of his height. Kevin is 5 feet, 2.5 inches (1.58 m) tall.

But Kevin doesn't mind being short. He tells lots of jokes about his size in his comedy routines. He believes people should use what they have, so he uses his short **stature**.

Kevin starred in the movie Jumanji: The Next Level *in 2019.*

Fun Facts

Kevin plays up his shortness in movies such as *Jumanji: Welcome to the Jungle* and *Jumanji: The Next Level*. In these movies, he plays **zoologist** Franklin "Mouse" Finbar.

HUMBLE BEGINNINGS

Kevin Hart was born on July 6, 1979, in Philadelphia, Pennsylvania, to Nancy Hart and Henry Witherspoon. Kevin and his older brother Robert were raised by their mom. Kevin did not see his dad much when he was a kid but grew closer to him as he got older.

Philadelphia, Pennsylvania

Kevin is joined by his brother, father, and actress Halle Berry on the Hollywood Walk of Fame in 2016.

When he was a teenager, Kevin got his first job selling shoes. His co-workers thought he was funny. They talked him into performing at an **amateur** comedy club. His jokes weren't good, but he loved doing stand-up comedy. He decided he could improve if he worked hard at it.

Fun Facts

Kevin wrote jokes based on his experiences traveling back and forth to work.

GETTING INTO COMEDY

Kevin's mom wanted him to go to college after high school. He tried community college, but he wanted to do comedy full time.

Kevin's mom said she would pay his rent for one year so he could try. But if he could not make it work, he would have to go to college. Kevin agreed.

Fun Facts

Kevin's mom wanted him to read his Bible, so she put the rent money in it but did not tell him. After not paying his rent for months, he finally opened his Bible and found the money.

Kevin had a slow start. He performed at small comedy clubs using the name "Lil' Kev." Not many people came to his shows. Most did not think he was funny. He tried copying other comedians, but that did not work either.

FINDING SUCCESS

Kevin found a **mentor** in **veteran** comedian Keith Robinson. Keith gave Kevin advice about his comedy shows. He told Kevin to perform using his own name instead of Lil' Kev. He showed Kevin that he could create jokes from his own real-life experiences and tough times.

Keith Robinson

Kevin took Keith's advice, and his career started to take off. He played a role in a TV **sitcom** in 2001. Then he starred in his first movie role in 2002. Other movies followed. His first televised comedy routine was on Comedy Central in 2004.

Kevin with actress Arnetia Walker, his co-star in The Big House

Kevin with the **cast** from The Big House

Fun Facts

When Kevin was 25 years old, he was given the starring role on a TV sitcom called *The Big House*. But it never caught on and was canceled after six episodes.

AT THE TOP

In 2009, Kevin began touring with his own comedy show called *I'm a Grown Little Man*. He released his first stand-up **album** by the same name. It was a huge success, and more soon followed.

Fun Facts

Kevin was awarded a star on the Hollywood Walk of Fame in 2016.

Kevin continues to star in movies. These include *Central Intelligence*, *Ride Along*, and *The Upside*.

Kevin starred with Dwayne Johnson in the 2016 movie Central Intelligence.

Kevin is also a **voice actor** for movies such as *The Secret Life of Pets*, *DC League of Super-Pets*, and *Captain Underpants*.

Kevin is also an author. He writes about his experiences and what he has learned from them. He wants to help other people achieve success. He also writes funny novels for kids.

In 2017, Kevin wrote a book about his life called I Can't Make This Up: Life Lessons.

FAMILY TIES

Some of Kevin's favorite times are movie nights with his children, even though he often falls asleep.

Kevin has four children: Heaven Leigh, Hendrix, Kenzo, and Kaori. His wife's name is Eniko Parrish. He has learned he has to work hard to keep these relationships strong.

Kevin and his wife, Eniko Parrish

Kevin attends the movie premiere for The Secret Life of Pets 2 *with his family in 2019.*

In 2019, Kevin was seriously injured in a car accident. It took him many months of hard work to recover. Now he appreciates life more. He is more thankful for his family and friends.

Actors Will Ferrell and Dwayne Johnson join Kevin at a celebration for him at the TCL Chinese Theatre in Hollywood, California, in 2019.

Kevin Hart talks a lot about making choices. His decision to learn the skills he needed, work hard, and not quit helped him become one of America's favorite comedians.

GLOSSARY

album (AL-buhm): A collection of recordings that is available for download, or as a CD or a record

amateur (A-muh-cher): Doing something for enjoyment rather than as a job

cast (KAST): The actors in a movie or TV show

comedian (kuh-MEE-dee-uhn): A person who tells jokes or funny stories in front of an audience

mentor (MEN-tawr): Someone who plays an important role in another person's life as a guide or teacher

producer (pruh-DOO-ser): A person who oversees the making of a film or television show

sitcom (SIT-kom): A TV show about a group of characters in funny situations

stature (STA-cher): A person's height

veteran (VEH-ter-uhn): A person with a lot of experience in a certain activity

voice actor (VOYS AK-ter): An actor who provides voices for characters in animated films

zoologist (zoh-OL-uh-jist): A person who studies animals and their behavior

INDEX

WEBSITES TO VISIT

https://kids.kiddle.co/Kevin_Hart

www.goodmorningamerica.com/culture/video/kevin-hart-talks-childrens-book-marcus-makes-big-84489194

www.aetv.com/videos/biography-kevin-hart

ABOUT THE AUTHOR

Samantha Bell lives with her family in the foothills of the Blue Ridge Mountains. She has four gray cats with a lot of attitude. When she's not writing, she likes to draw, hike, and visit new places.

Crabtree Publishing

crabtreebooks.com 800-387-7650

Copyright © 2025 Crabtree Publishing

All rights reserved. No part of this publication may be reproduced, stored in a retrieval system or be transmitted in any form or by any means, electronic, mechanical, photocopying, recording, or otherwise, without the prior written permission of Crabtree Publishing.

Written by: Samantha Bell
Designed by: Kathy Walsh
Series Development: James Earley
Proofreader: Melissa Boyce
Educational Consultant: Marie Lemke M.Ed.
Production manager: Candice Campbell

Hardcover: 978-1-0398-3908-3
Paperback: 978-1-0398-3993-9
Ebook (pdf): 978-1-0398-4065-2
Epub: 978-1-0398-4137-6

Printed in the U.S.A./CP082026

Published in Canada
Crabtree Publishing
616 Welland Ave.
St. Catharines, Ontario
L2M 5V6

Published in the United States
Crabtree Publishing
347 Fifth Ave
Suite 1402-145
New York, NY 10016

Library and Archives Canada Cataloguing in Publication
Available at Library and Archives Canada

Library of Congress Cataloging-in-Publication Data
Available at the Library of Congress

Photographs: Shutterstock, Newscom: Cover, Title pg, Backgrounds: Jim Ruymen/UPIviaNewscom , Anna Davidovskaya, StockAppeal, Vector Tradition, Miloje; p 7, 11, 14, 19, 21: Vector Tradition; p 5, 17: StockAppeal; p 3: DFree; p 4: gotpap/starmaxinc.com; p 5: Birdie Thompson/AdMedia/SplashNews; p 6: Faiz Zaki; p 7: Sony Pictures; 8: Marco Rubino, Popartic; p 9: Albert L. Ortega; p 10: Tom Rodriguez; p 11: MZ1; p 12: LCD/SplashNews; p 13; JLC/ZOJ; p 14: JLC/ZOJ; p 15: Kathy Hutchins; p16: JcOlivera/Sipa USA; p 17: Ga Fullner; p 18: BARBARA BINSTEIN; p 19: Craig Sjodin; p 20: JLC/ZOJ; p 21: Featureflash Photo Agency; p 22: NEW LINE CINEMA via Newscom; p 23: Illumination Entertainment/Universal Pictures; p 24: Johnny Louis; p 25: Ga Fullner; p 26: Xavier Collin/Image Press Agency; p 27: Kathy Hutchins; p 28: Jim Ruymen; p 29: Picture Happy Photos/imageSPACE